CW00894152

DISSECT MY FRAGILE BRAIN

KIM YUDELOWITZ

Time is an Ocean Publications

Time is an Ocean Publications
An Imprint of **write**_ahead_
Lonsdale Road
Wolverhampton, WV3 0DY

First Printed Edition written and published
by **Time is an Ocean Publications, 2021**
Text copyright © **Kim Yudelowitz 2021**
The right of Kim Yudelowitz to be identified as
the author of this work has been asserted by her in accordance
with the Copyright, Designs and Patents Act 1988.
All images within this book are copyright
© **Kim Yudelowitz 2021** except where shown

TO MY BELOVED DAD WHOM I
LOVE MORE THAN ANYTHING
AND MISS EVERY DAY

Leor Joseph Yudelowitz: 10 July 1955 – 12 March 2013

FOREWORD

In an exploration of her loss, Kim invites you to ride the waves of grief with her in this, her debut book *Dissect My Fragile Brain*. These pages of poetry scrutinise the many emotions that come with grief. Kim delves deep into three specific sections, **Love**, **Loss** and **Life** which all connote grief in some way…

Grief is something that never goes away, but is something we carry with us forever. I will forever carry my dad with me, and treasure the times we had, but also mourn the times we didn't have. My family and I were robbed, and the gaping hole that sits in our lives is permanent.

There is a misconception with grief, that *"time heals all wounds"* and that with time things get better. I'd like to shut this misconception down. If anything, with time, the pain gets stronger, because it is a longer amount of time since you were last with the person you have lost… the last time you heard their voice and the last time you hugged. Time allows the wound to gape wide open. You learn to live with that gaping hole because you don't have a choice.

One story I'd like to share with you all is a story my mum told me, and one I will treasure for life:

One day mum found an empty carton of milk in the fridge, which frustrated her so she went to tell dad off. Dad replied: *"But there is milk in there, I'll show you"* and he proceeded to tip the carton over her head, and a trickle of milk dropped onto mum's head.

"See I told you it wasn't empty," dad exclaimed with a grin. This captures the true essence of my beloved dad: intelligent, cheeky and humorous.

To my dad, **Leor Joseph Yudelowitz**, I will love and miss you forever. You were always there for me during what can only be described as a difficult, confusing time in my life and I just wish you could see how far I've come.

Who would have thought your little *Cheeso* would be writing poetry!

Thank you for being you, and only you, just like when you wore jeans to your wedding. I will channel all I have of you inside me (which I've heard is a lot) with all I have and continue your legacy. Your name **Leor**, translates from Hebrew to English as *Light…* and dad, you have been an eternal lights in our lives.

> *"Touched down in the land of the Delta Blues*
> *In the middle of the pouring rain"*

From our song that we listened to together so many times. ***Walking In Memphis*** by Marc Cohn.

Kim Yudelowitz
February 2021

LOSS

Loss is something that is inevitable in life, but something we are most ill equipped to face.
When that loss happens prematurely, it seems unjust.
Writing is my way of dealing with the significant loss that I have had in my life.

Years have passed but the love and cherished memories are engrained within me

Discover every inch of me
Dissect my fragile brain
Unearth my inhibitions, reveal my secrets
Dig up the skeletons in my closet
Blow away the dust that's concealing my affliction
Explore my thoughts and feelings
Uncover my sentiments and what is preventing the
healing
Pick at me like a flower
Watch me grow and bloom
Until the next wave of sadness looms

A world shattered
Ruptured my equilibrium
An explosion in my heart
Life as I know it faded into smoke
Back to square one
Starting from scratch
By putting the pieces back together

Fragmented feelings
obtaining me
And possessing
the thoughts
occupying my mind
Like a tenant
With no means
To leave anytime soon

Filled with dread
My mind runs wild
Apprehending the worst
Fearing the best
Possibilities of solace and heartbreak
Stuck in a domain of dismay
The prospect of losing you
Is hard to swallow

A smile I can sustain
Until I remember
That it's you
That I've lost
And all the pain
And sadness
Comes crashing down on me
Like a thunder storm

Waiting for the pain to subside
For the pulsating sensation to stop
Yet I think I've acclimatised to it
Adapted to the cavity that glares
Me in the face
To never be restored again

The reminder of you taints my smile
And sends pain through my veins
I hold on to the sadness like a souvenir
that you left for me as a gesture
to not let me forget
That I'm falling apart

Opened a door
To a room full of emotions
one enters with fear
When they discover
My fragile brain
Embellished within the walls
And notice the draws
Piled high with pain

A swarm of teardrops roll down my face
And evaporate into yesterday's air
While searching for their destination of tomorrow
Sliding down a narrow path
Eluding any obstacles they may encounter
In the flaws of my skin, and brokenness of my heart
A journey of pursuit, an expedition for meaning
A crave by virtue of sentiment
That reminds me of my own

A dark matter
pervades my mind
When a thought of you
Enlightens me
And makes me think
Of everything that we had
And what could have been

Pain lingers like an unwanted odour

A presence so scarce yet so prominent
I dwell on the last time I saw you and
held your fragile hands
Lifeless and restricted in movement
I squeeze them
in the hope to reinstall strength
A trauma enunciated by my memories
that I see ever so clearly
no missing fragments or gaps
Conspicuous in detail
like a tape replaying on my mind
How does one shut out the past
when it lingers like an unwanted odour?

Engulfed in feelings
Consumed by ideas
Caught up in the concept
That time is supposed to heal
But as time has progressed
I am stagnant
Awaiting the moment
Someday
When we meet again

A river of uncertainty
That flows like
A well recited poem
Only to be obstructed
By a rock
That sits in the stream ahead
And hinders my thoughts

There are monsters under my bed

And demons in my head
They cling to me like glue
And scrutinise my every move
Yet there's something about them
That makes wonder
If they are deceivers
And the real monster
Is actually, me

A path left untouched

Footprints not trodden
Your presence dissipated
A long and winding road
full of memories
That I am bereft of

A contorted mind

Irrational speculation
Incoherent assumptions
That hit me
Like a gust of wind
And persists
With vengeance

A heavy heart
Weighing several tonnes
It slows me down
But I don't have enough hands
To carry this much pain

A shiver runs down my spine
A paralysing sensation
A destruction in my body
Catalysed by the thought of you
A reminder of the
infinite detriment

Submerged in darkness

I'm susceptible to the gloom
A fog of obscurity inundates me
With the light being blocked
by the endless sorrow
That yearns for your return
Before the melancholy
Eternally remains

A bleak morning

Rain droplets slide down the window
I think of you with a heavy heart
On a dreary day with a lack
flowers aching in the wind
I get up with a broken heart
and shattered hope
calling out on a dream that will never
Be mine

It's all fun and games
Until it's all pain and suffering
Broken beyond repair
Hands full of despair
Anguish seeping through my fingers
As I clench my fists ever so tightly
To try make myself disappear

Left me like a stone
A hard exterior by appearance
But crumbling beneath
An obvious trauma
Illuminated by a broken heart
That blinds me
And leaves me gasping for air
When you're the one
In need of resuscitating

The loss of happy family times still hurts deep inside

Tangled in a web of disarray

Caught in a netting of living in the past
Clinging to the memories I so want to forget
But the complexity of my pain takes control
As the weaving of the entanglement
overrides my strength
And I'm stuck exactly where I began

Obliterate the memories

Dismiss all the conversations
Draw a blank through the pictures
That hang on the walls of my mind
And constantly remind me
Of the emptiness I feel without you
The desolation that echoes
from your absence

Drowned in fear

Engrossed in the black hole
kaleidoscopic emotions
A magnitude of colours
Fore-fronting my feelings
Motioning through the motley crew

An absence

That remains
in the background
Of an intense destiny
mirroring an emptiness
Solitude and seclusion
A fortitude of angst
That has become persistent

A contorted mind
Irrational speculation
Incoherent assumptions
That hit me
Like a gust of wind
And persists
With vengeance

A shadow
Dragging the world behind them
That creeps up on you
In the darkest of moments
Reminding you of the pain you've endured
And all that is left to come

Faint and obscured memories
Of a past life
Encompassing forgotten feelings
And new beginnings
A preoccupied mind
Yet I still wallow
In my tears

Surrendered to my darkest thoughts
I'm lost in the shadows
Surrounded by my broken dreams
Confined by the detriment of my desires
Perplexed by my damaged imagination
And the love that slowly dissolves away

19

An over active mind
And a restless imagination
That dances with the shadows
And comes to life in the darkness
Thriving off fragmented memories
And morbid thoughts

Ferocious waters
Struggling to stay afloat
On the shore of an endless world
With the waves
Sending symphonies through my ears
Entering below the surface
Where I'm
Battered and bruised

Absent from my body
And estranged from my mind
While I watch the sky spill with colour
And embellish myself with tears
To conceal my scars

A downpour of sorrow
That elucidates the air
Dissipating slowly
While the wind moans
And harmonises
With the permanent pain
in my voice

A cloud of darkness resides
above my head
The taste of despair
lingers in my mouth
Melancholy blurs my vision
And all I can see is the pain of yesterday
Like a broken clock stuck in a moment
Searching through the residue that remains
A stationary car stuck at a red light
A perpetual feeling engrained in me
All that we can hold on to
Is the residue that remains

Constant nightmares

Susceptible to the darkness
That emerges from my fractured brain
Partaking in fear
And fuelling the angst
That comes hand in hand with
The endless horror that plays in my mind
And corrupts my thoughts

Stagnant and still

I'm stuck in a motion
Inconsolable and torn
I'm broken internally
Half of the person I use to be
No recollection of feeling whole
Unsure of the person
In the reflection of the mirror
For they can scream
Whereas I only cry

A fire in my head
I'm suffocating
A ruptured heart
And a fractured mind
I need time
No
I need space
Alone
In the open air
Serene and quiet
No
It's chaotic and loud
An incessant beat
Blaring in my chest

Searching for peace
But bombarded with noise
Of a deadly silence
With explicit intentions
That breaks me in two
So I face an interior conflict
I'm between two minds
And one of them is out to get me

A brokenness
Fractured dreams and desires
Sprawled across the floor
Shattered into pieces so tiny
They're unrecognisable and unfamiliar
To my sharp eyes
That loom above, attempting to repair
My collapsed mind

Lost in the light of my imagination
Caught in a web of fantasy
Blinded by my delusions
That leave me
Unaware of the fabrication
That's masking my inhibitions
To be destructive and damaging

Turmoil and treacherous

The void you left gets bigger
And acts as an indicator
For all that you'll miss
And the gaping hole
That sits in my heart
Will also be present
In the room

A life sentence

A verdict set in stone
Without a choice
To object to the significant loss
That accompanies us
While we cling on to
Cell bars
Screaming for a way out

In a better place
They say
No longer in pain
They say
But have you ever stopped to wonder
The place those of us who are left are in
Or the pain we now pursue
And bear the brunt of
For life

A persistent darkness clings to my body
It encapsulates me
and lingers like a cloud
Waiting for it to pass but
it haunts me like a curse

Defined by tragedy

Represented by brokenness
Shaped by the events that have taken place
Sculpted my mind
Lay the foundations for my soul
To be consumed by your absence
Until we meet again

LOVE

*Love connotes loss, as we would not feel the significant loss
unless there was love involved.
The love I feel for my dad is something that will never go away,
and something that I will carry with me for the rest of my life.*

Such happy memories of family, love and life together

At night
You come alive in my mind
And dance to the tune
Of my imagination
Catapulting
And propelling
Through thoughts
As I drift off
To sleep

It's my love for you
That haunts me most
Lurking in the shadows
Pervading my body
And making their stay
Perpetual

A gorgeous demeanour
That awakens a room
Dreamy and compliant eyes
That absorb me
And force me
To do nothing but smile

A harmonious song
You sang along
To the sound of my heart
And danced to the sound
Of it falling apart

Full of emptiness
A hollowness that exists
Purely in place of my love
That's devoid of sentiment
And unwilling
To fill the void

An unwillingness to let go
Clinging on to all that was had
At least I've learnt for next time
To keep my heart closer to my chest
And not on the edge of my sleeve

A vision of ecstasy

A reminder of what I love
And what I've lost
That dawdles in the distance
But is out of my reach

Embraced by a tirade

Of everlasting love
And never ending passion
Provoked by the memories
Enhanced by time
A hole in my heart
A vacancy in my dreams

Transfixed in a moment
Enchanted by an instant
Captivated by the time
The darkest nights
Were lessened
With your voice
And soothed with
Your words

They say time is a healer
But that's exactly
what I'm afraid of
Months and days passing
Only to become like a grain of sand
Slipping through your fingers

It's funny
How all of a sudden
A tender touch
Becomes a cold shoulder
And blissful happiness
Turns into a river of tears

Profound love today
Becomes the buried
wound of tomorrow
That's masked by
A laugh
And later
Evolves into a cry

Such porcelain eyes

Kind and warm
putting everyone at ease
I just wonder
What they carried
And what discernment
They kept to themselves

It's a sad day

When I remember
I can no longer see your smile
Or hold your hand
While others take that sight
And touch
For granted
And I cling on
To the recollection of you
For dear life

Time can elapse

And clocks can transpire
But my love for you
Will not expire
And the memories
Will sit poignantly
In my mind

Rich with desire

A constant flame
Keeping my fighting spirit alive
While I grapple
With the hostility
Of my feelings towards you

A brokenness within a smile
Pain pouring from the lips
Each layer of skin
revealing a collapsed thought
Cracks on the surface
depicting the void
That is so palpable
Something strong
is needed to reattach
But that is… you

Feelings just as prominent
Pain just as raw
For your sake
I sincerely hope
No one breaks your heart
Like you did
Mine

A light shimmers
On the water
While cradling the moon
Held ever so tightly
Like a mother holding a child
Circumspect to abandon
What is being kept
Close to her heart

Always together for eternity

A vision of ecstasy
A reminder of what I love
And what I've lost
That dawdles in the distance
But is out of my reach

Transfixed in a moment
Enchanted by an instant
Captivated by the time
The darkest nights
Were lessened
With your voice
And soothed with
Your words

Sunken dreams

I'm immune to the nightmares
The clearest of views is all I see
The sun shining ever so brightly
So picturesque, like a photo on a postcard
A gentle wind hits my face
I close my eyes
and transport back to our time together
with endless laughs and prolonged smiles
Memories encompassed in every corner of my mind
All sadness abandoned
All pain buried

Averting attention

Bypassing reflection
Thoughts of you
That waft through me
Like a cloud of smoke
Only to disappear
Into thin air

Wooden smiles

A brave face
Masking her tearful eyes
That glistened like the morning frost
A reminder
Of what she cannot forget

You live in my dreams
Entering during my
hours of delusion
Bearing gifts of solace and smiles
While my eyes
Are squeezed shut

A symphony ever so silent
That I hear every morning
And every night
That reverberates through my ears
Down into my heart of misery
And sits there
Allowing me to feel your presence

A presence so infectious

A smile so contagious
immune to negativity
peers and acquaintances drawn to you
like a magnet
A reassuring voice
a gentle hand
So nonchalant and serene
no worries or any issues
Like bees surrounding a beautiful flower
We flocked to you for advice and guidance
A pristine mind and a golden heart
I long for your Midas touch
An eternal flame, an infinite light
That sheds encouragement
to my everyday fight

A crooked smile
A deceitful laugh
Happiness that disappears
in a puff of smoke
There's always more to a person
Than what meets the eye

I'll chase your shadow forever
And search the world
for your footsteps
For I want to leave an imprint
Like the one you left on me

Sadness worn like a veil
Lifting momentarily
When I resort
To enveloping myself
Into the time
When you were still here

A you-shaped space in my heart
That enlarges as time goes on
The territory belongs to you
Irreplaceable and beyond repair
Love erupts through the emptiness
And journeys around my body
Resulting in tears

A bed of roses
That sweet smell of clove
That resonates in my mind with love,
With you
But then I see the thorns sticking out
That I have to carefully navigate through
Each change of direction faced with a different
obstacle
Following the path I thought I knew
Only to be punctured by a thorn
And change my life forever

I still feel remnants of you
Buried and absorbed inside of me
Flowing through my body
And rippling around my brain
But uncovering the vestige is bitter sweet
A grin that results in tears
As I remember the residue persists
Because you are not here

Coerced by my wild brain
A chaotic utopia
That draws me to you
Like a moth to a flame
Yearning for your presence
And a blink of your eyes
A compulsion that I can't control
The same one that left me in pieces
And leaves me
Mourning something that I lost
Eight years ago

Whispers from the trees

And screams from the wind
Regardless of the weather
The sound of you
In my ears
Is always welcome

A tirade of feelings

That sings a song of sensitivity
with sweetness alongside bitterness
And follows me like an apparition
Pursing my susceptibility
Whilst we sing together

Unfamiliar territory

And obscure emotions
Your smile is a catalyst
For a stampede of happiness
That infiltrates me
And takes me to a better place

Imprisoned by your memory

Sentenced to the pain for life
You're trapped in my heart
And I'm captured in a cell
Hoping one day
You'll lead me to the light

Such enclosed feelings

Suffocating in my own thoughts
Inundated with reflection of our time together
An exploration into my brain
And the underlying emotions
That resonate with you
An the eternal flame you burn within
My heart

Inadvertently together

Bonded by the blood and DNA we share
A stream that collides collectively
Consolidating us as one
Bound together
Til death do us part
And thereafter

Left to pick up the pieces
And reassemble the remains
I'll sew them in to a blanket of pain
And hope that one day
I can love again

Vivid dreams
Based on faint memories
That are so in reach yet
so unattainable
they taunt me
With hope and belief
that makes me sustain all feelings
But then arrives fear and despair
Holding hands while they embody me
As I drift back to sleep

LIFE

While we wrestle with the pain of the loss, we also celebrate the life of my dad and everything he was. His legacy is continued by myself and my brother, as he is within us forever.

I miss cuddling and being close to dad so very much

It comes in waves
Gentle and calm
Ferocious and turbulent
There is no in between
Just a fluctuation
Of one end of the spectrum
To the other
From a dark red
To a light yellow
And serenity is restored

Head in the clouds
I'm immersed into the sky
A tumultuous journey
With the wind crashing against me
I'm as fragile as a leaf
But numb to any emotion
So engrossed in feelings
It is all that surrounds me
And I'm transparent to pain
It flows through me like a stream
And stays within me like a scar

It takes time
To make peace with the events
that have occurred
And pervaded my existence
Brought a permanent cloud
that reigns above my head
And awaits its cue
To open the void
And continue its journey
One instant
That changes you forever
A moment secured in time
Engrained in you indefinitely
The seasons may change
And the flowers will prosper
But I'm locked in this mind-set
And I can't find the key

A hard exterior
Solid as armour
Strength of steel
Until someone mentions your name
Then the cracks begin to show
My kryptonite corroding my shell
Revealing that I've been
hollow inside
All along

When the facade starts to wear
And the veneer begins to crumble
I'll allow my vulnerabilities to shine through
And unmask
The inadequacies
That have been tightly concealed

Caught in an idea
Captured in a belief
And ruminating in assumptions
Of insincerity and deceit
But underneath the surface
It's important to divulge
That I am more than enough

A pain felt so deeply
The discomfort oozes out the other side
A reminder of what
I've been through
A nostalgia of that time
Can't get rid of the memory
It's like it's engraved in my mind
Even when it's healed
There's still an everlasting throb
An inconsistent sensation
A reminder of you

So alone on the surface

so accompanied through the cracks
Absorbed in thoughts
distracted by the noise
So much noise yet so immersed in silence
A chorus of voices congregate in my ears
Volume and pitch rising
like the sun at the crack of dawn
Giving me direction, advice
and a small amount of affection
So attainable yet so far out of reach
Unable to persevere
I'm paralysed at the core
And become like a dead flower
that's been picked at and forgotten

A vacancy
Like at a motel on the high road
With an incessant neon light
That acts as a catalyst
For a tingling through my senses
Sparking feelings of resent
Towards your absence

Amid the noise
Be present in the silence
Vicariously enjoying a sense of nothing
Solitude and detachment
Present in your own space
Avoiding the commotion
Escaping the pandemonium
And endure the harmony
Of your natural reticence

L'Chaim – to Life… always our champion

Awoken dreams inside of me
Ignited by the devastation
Enthralled by the woe
But when will I turn the page
Onto the blank canvas that awaits me?
And accept the cookies
Without accepting the monster

Moving daintily amongst
a flower garden
Prancing through chrysanthemums
And eucalyptus trees
Ravishing at the beauty
Only to discover
thorns within roses
And rottenness within the air

Spreading my wings
To attain a new chapter
With blank pages and fresh starts
Yet I'm permanently plagued
With the thought of you
In the back of my mind

Caught in an idea
Captured in a belief
And ruminating in assumptions
Of insincerity and deceit
But underneath the surface
It's important to divulge
That I am more than enough

Spending too

many days in my head
Ruminating and contemplating
Hoping that one day
the thoughts will be dispelling
As I work on fighting
the hardest opponent
Me, myself and I

Old wounds

Re-emerging through the obscurity
of the night
Back with vengeance
And reincarnated
With a mind of its own

A path left untouched

Footprints not trodden
Your presence dissipated
A long and winding road
full of memories
That I am bereft of

A river of uncertainty

That flows like
A well recited poem
Only to be obstructed
By a rock
That sits in the stream ahead
And hinders my thoughts

Engulfed in feelings

Consumed by ideas
Caught up in the concept
That time is supposed to heal
But as time has progressed
I am stagnant
Awaiting the moment
Someday
When we meet again

Moving between partitions

Searching for answers
Questioning the sequence of events
Equanimity is the only option
Until I re enter
A sense of brokenness
And throw myself against the wall
Wishing you would come back

A sphere of instability

A dismal rotation
The world circling me
like paint down a plug hole
Only for the loop
To start over
once again

Mournful of the past

Mindful of the present
And fearful of the future
To become a distant memory
Like a rock that has sunk
To the bottom of the ocean

When the facade starts to wear

And the veneer begins to crumble
I'll allow my vulnerabilities to shine through
And unmask
The inadequacies
That have been tightly concealed

It's a fight with no winner

A battle with no ending
An unresolved equilibrium
So I'll just keep talking to the stars
In the clearest of night
And allow myself to feel again

Feelings that I can't ignore
Estranged from the person
I use to know
Like old flowers in a vase
It's time to let go

Trembling with fear
I'm awakened with angst
And alive with dismay
So out of control
Yet I'm in the driver's seat
With the choice in my hands
To decide my fate

An undercurrent of animosity

Inclinations of bitterness
The elephant in the room
That we choose to ignore
But how do you ignore an empty chair
Or a photograph with one less person
A hole that gapes open
And not even glue
Can sustain keeping it shut

Spending too

many days in my head
Ruminating and contemplating
Hoping that one day
the thoughts will be dissipating
As I work on fighting
the hardest opponent
Me, myself and I

Always part of him as he is part of me

Awoken with fantasy

I still ruminate the possibilities
Of beautiful complexities
And scenarios that may occur
One day
When the morning sun retains
Its strength
And the clouds begin to shift

Gracefully surrendering

As I'm swept into delirium
Eradicated of all control
And left to fend for myself
Inhibiting a chaotic mind
Faced with negligence
and disappointment
As I try to regulate
My tempestuous brain

Infiltrated thoughts

Like an army
Bombarding through me
And transporting me away
Through the many suns and moons
Until my pain is camouflaged
And my comrades are dead

A secluded mind

Isolated by my own thoughts
Hidden away from civilisation
Sticking close to those I can trust
Me myself and I
The ones who aware of the fragility of life
And the pain of death

Induced madness

Divulged in insanity
Mauling at the remaining stability
That sits deep within my brain
In a complex area
So acute and out of reach
My lunacy will have to suffice

Defeated and deflated

Been through the wars
Trampled on and walked over
But still here to tell the tale
A tale of woes that is
About the massive hole that I feel
In your absence
A void that can never be filled
A jigsaw that can never be completed

Relentlessly trying
To be the person I use to be
That vanished with you
Disappeared into thin air
And evaporated with everyone else's pain
Now I claw at the remains
Scratching at the surface to try redeem
Who I was
Before I hit rock bottom
And haven't moved since

Inadequacy transpires
To new heights
Floating through paucity
Staring into space
One that I once admired
Now holding on to
New aspirations
And looking ahead
To new sights

Fixated on a moment

I'm lost in the past
And fearful of the future
When the blossoms bloom
And the flower buds open
Along with more change
To commence

Trying to stay afloat

My thoughts of you act as a life jacket
Grasping above the unknown
Retreating to normality
Before I hold my breath
And transport myself back to reality
Where you no longer exist
And I'm drowning

Unaware of the fragility
That accompanies
The wrath of my emotions
When I recollect
How seldom
You think of me

Burning temptations
I'm alive with sensation
But hollow of affection
That I hope to redeem
When the fire goes out

Painting the town blue

My sadness prevails
always finding a way to creep out
Like a sieve
Reminding me of the pain I've felt
And what is to come

As fragile as glass

I've been chipped around the edges
Taken some knocks, but the marks have faded
Disappeared into the air
Absorbed and perished without warning
Though the pain and anguish
Is yet to depart

Reluctant to let go
Bursting through the cage
That's held me so tight
Enclosed myself in a darkened space
Isolated by my thoughts
Nothing went beyond the four walls
Of the segregated confinement
That left me feeling lonesome
Until I found my freedom
And flew away
Like a bird

It's a fight with no winner
A battle with no ending
An unresolved equilibrium
So I'll just keep talking to the stars
In the clearest of night
And allow myself to feel again

A void so prominent
I fear
If I surrender
It will swallow me up whole

Maybe one day
I'll surrender to the
Weight of pain
That shifts like
A tide
And steadily
Floats away

I'm clinging on to each moment
When we were together
And nothing else mattered
I live iteratively
Grasping at all that remains
In the hope that one day
You'll come back to me

Me and my beautiful family…

Meet the Author

Dissect My Fragile Brain is written by **Kim Yudelowitz** and published by *Time is an Ocean Publications*.

Kim is from Mill Hill in North London. Both her parents are from Johannesburg, South Africa. She has an older brother, Jake who she considers as one of her best friends.

Kim studied Comparative Literature at Queen Mary University of London, where she earned a Bachelor of Arts degree. She started writing poetry to deal with grief and process her varied emotions when she was 20. She maintains a social media account on Instagram *@poetrybykim* where she posts her poems in both written and spoken form. She hopes to pursue a career in publishing and write a novel, when she finally learns to write more than a few words in one go!

Kim enjoys contemporary art exhibitions and is an avid reader of thrillers and classic literature and a lover of sausage dogs (dachshunds)!

Dad was always pointing to the future… one day I will reach out and touch his hand again

Help dealing with grief and loss

**gr•ef
encounter**

Grief Encounter
Grief Encounter's mission is to give every child and young person access to the best possible support following the death of someone close.
They work closely with individuals, families, schools and professionals to offer a way through the anxiety, fear and isolation so often caused by grief.
Their services include:
One-to-one counselling
Group workshops
Music, Art and drama therapy
Residentials and Family Fun Days
A National, free and confidential helpline called grieftalk offering web chat services
A dedicated Trauma Team for support following a sudden or traumatic bereavement.
Accredited training courses and webinars for professionals. They can be found at:
https://www.griefencounter.org.uk

talking through the taboo

Let's Talk About Loss

Let's Talk About Loss, a safe space to talk through taboos and address the reality of losing someone close to you when you are young.

A 2018 survey found that 16 to 29-year-olds are the age group most likely to bottle up their grief and not talk about it, with 24% saying they *"kept it to themselves"* when suffering a bereavement.

Let's Talk About Loss runs peer-led meet up groups in cities across the UK for young people aged 18 to 35 who have been bereaved at any stage. Find your local meet up group here at the dedicated website: https://letstalkaboutloss.org

Registered charity number: 1172763

The Good Grief Trust

The Good Grief Trust exists to help all those affected by grief in the UK.

It aims to find the bereaved, acknowledge their grief and provide reassurance, a virtual hand of friendship and ongoing support

Their vision is to bring all bereavement services together, to ensure that everyone receives the support they need to move forward with their lives

They aim to encourage talking about grief in a more honest, straightforward way, help to make the pain a little more bearable for those at the early stages and offer inspiration and hope to the bereaved further along their own grief journey.

https://www.thegoodgrieftrust.org

MIND

MIND provides advice and support to empower anyone experiencing a mental health problem.

MIND aims to empower people to understand their condition and the choices available to them through the following:

Infoline offers callers confidential help for the price of a local call.

A Legal Line provides information on mental health related law to the public, service users, family members/carers, mental health professionals and mental health advocates.

Award-winning publications and website, now certified by the Information Standard.

https://www.mind.org.uk

Acknowledgements

I'd like to thank Nic for this incredible opportunity. His passion and dedication to his work is mind blowing and the fortuity he has given me is something I will forever be grateful for.

Thank you to Instagram for allowing us to find each other, and not only allowing us to collaborate on this book together, but for finding me a new friend. Thank you for believing in my words enough to want to publish them. It means more than you know.

A big thank you to my family and my friends for sticking by me no matter what, putting up with my silly jokes and down moments, and allowing me to be myself.

To my brother Jake, who is the most selfless, kind and genuine person I know; you have never let me down and go above and beyond for me, and I am eternally grateful to you.

Thank you to you, the reader, for reading my words and embracing my grief. Thank you for allowing me to reach new people and make grief a less taboo topic.

And finally thank you to my mum and dad, for bringing me into this world first and foremost, but for being there for me through my darkest times.

My mum is the strongest person I'll ever know. Her resilience is something I can only hope to have one day.

She is my rock, my shoulder to cry on. These last few years would have been even tougher without you, and I couldn't be more thankful to have you by my side.

Thank you to my dad for being my never-ending light, I love you and miss you.

Kim Yudelowitz
February 2021

Also by Time is an Ocean

The Hill - Songs and Poems of Darkness and Light
Another Hill - Songs and Poems of Love and Theft
Asian Voices
Asian Voices - the Director's Cut
Blood in the Cracks
Don't Look Down
Luminance - Words for a World Gone Wrong
Death in Grimsby
Bones
Hot Metal – Poems from the Print Room
Poets Don't Lie
Contacts
The Man's a Tart
Western Skies
Reality Cornflakes
A Moon Magnetized This Screeching Bird
The Arbitrary Fractals of an Oracle

Printed in Great Britain
by Amazon